My First Picture Encyclopedia

Show Me
THE
CONTINENTS

by Pamela Dell

Consultant:

Harold Perkins, PhD

Associate Professor of Geography

Ohio University

CAPSTONE PRESS

a capstone imprint

A+ Books are published by Capstone Press,
1710 Roe Crest Drive, North Mankato, Minnesota 56003.
www.capstonepub.com

Library of Congress Cataloging-in-Publication Data
Cataloging-in-publication information is on file with the Library of Congress.
ISBN 978-1-4765-0114-7 (library binding)
ISBN 978-1-4765-3344-5 (paper over board)
ISBN 978-1-4765-3348-3 (paperback)
ISBN 978-1-4765-3352-0 (eBook PDF)

Editorial Credits
Jill Kalz, editor; Heidi Thompson, designer; Svetlana Zhurkin, media researcher; Laura Manthe, production specialist

Photo Credits
iStockphotos: Keith Szafranski, 15 (bottom); National Geographic Stock: Bill Curtsinger, 15 (top); Newscom: Kyodo, 15 (middle); Shutterstock: 2009fotofriends, 21 (top), Achim Baque, 23 (bottom), Alexander Dvorak, 9 (top), Alfonso de Tomas, 4, Andrew Zarivny, 21 (middle), Anton Balazh, 14, Anton Ivanov, 19 (top), AridOcean, 20, Artography, 29 (bottom), Daniel Prudek, 29 (top), Davor Pukljak, 16, deb22, 7 (top), Denis Tabler, 9 (bottom), Dimitrios, 12 (bottom), Dmitry Saparov, 17 (top), Donya Nedomam, 31 (bottom), Dr. Morley Read, 17 (middle), 19 (bottom), Eric Isselee, back cover (bottom right), 8 (bottom), 9 (middle left), 12 (middle), 18 (bottom), 27 (top), 30 (bottom), Fabio Mancino Photography, 13 (top), fivespots, 23 (middle), Four Oaks, 27 (bottom), Galyna Andrushko, 25 (top), Greg Ward NZ, 8 (top), Grin Maria, 11, Jan Martin Will, cover (bottom left), Jan Miko, 22 (top), Johan Swanepoel, back cover (bottom left), 10, Jorge Felix Costa, 12 (top), Kokhanchikov, cover (top), 1 (top), Leonello Calvetti, 28, Lightspring, 6, 24, LysFoto, 19 (middle), mironov, 30 (top), mmmm, 27 (middle), N Mrtgh, 7 (middle), Natalia Bratslavsky, 22 (middle), neelsky, 29 (middle), Nikolai Tsvetkov, 13 (bottom), Odua Images (torn paper), cover, 1, Pal Teravagimov, cover (Everest), 25 (bottom), Pecold, 25 (middle), Peder Digre, 22 (bottom), RCPPhoto, 30 (middle), rebvt, 17 (bottom), Richard Cavalleri, 26 (top), Sapsiwai, cover (bottom right), 26 (bottom), Smileus, 8 (middle), StevanZZ, back cover (top), 9 (middle right), Tanawat Pontchour, 18 (middle), Tristan Tan, cover (cacao), Volina, cover (back), back cover (back), 1 (back), 2–3 (back), Waj, 31 (top), WDG Photo, 13 (middle), Yaromir, 18 (top), Yuri Yavnik, 31 (middle); Wikipedia: John O'Neill, 7 (bottom)

Note to Parents, Teachers, and Librarians
My First Picture Encyclopedias provide an early introduction to reference materials for young children. These accessible, visual encyclopedias support literacy development by building subject-specific vocabularies and research skills. Stimulating format, inviting content, and phonetic aids assist and encourage young readers.

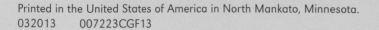
Printed in the United States of America in North Mankato, Minnesota.
032013   007223CGF13

Table of Contents

What Is a Continent?

A continent is a huge area of land. Earth has seven continents. From smallest to largest, they are Australia, Europe, Antarctica, South America, North America, Africa, and Asia. The continents share certain features. But they're also special in their own ways.

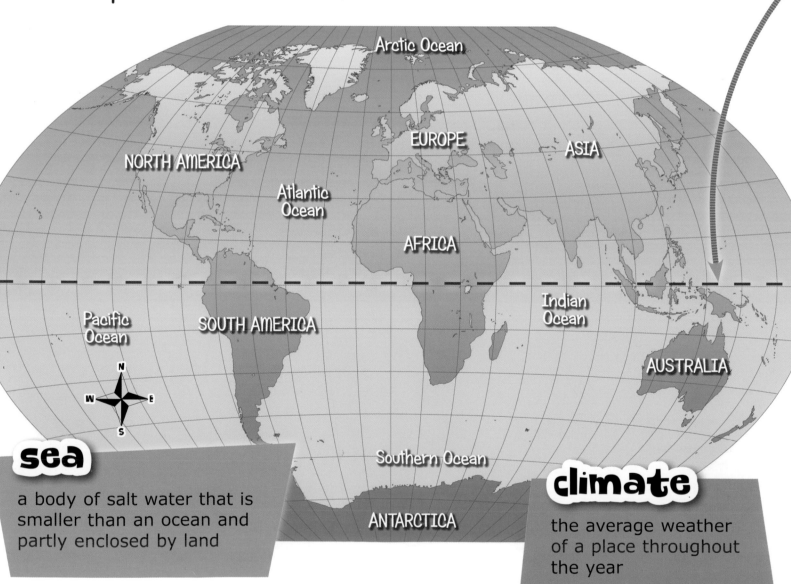

Arctic Ocean

NORTH AMERICA

EUROPE

ASIA

Atlantic Ocean

AFRICA

Pacific Ocean

SOUTH AMERICA

Indian Ocean

AUSTRALIA

Southern Ocean

ANTARCTICA

sea
a body of salt water that is smaller than an ocean and partly enclosed by land

climate
the average weather of a place throughout the year

4

equator

an imaginary east-west line that circles Earth at its middle; it lies halfway between the South Pole and the North Pole

ocean

a very large area of salt water; oceans cover nearly three-fourths of the planet; from smallest to largest, they are the Arctic, Southern, Indian, Atlantic, and Pacific oceans

supercontinent

a giant continent that many scientists believe broke into smaller continents, which moved away from each other; often called Pangaea

hemisphere

one half of Earth; the equator divides the northern and southern hemispheres, while the prime meridian and the international date line divide the eastern and western hemispheres

North Pole

the northernmost point on Earth; the North Pole lies in the Arctic Ocean, not on a continent

latitude lines

imaginary lines that run east and west on both sides of the equator

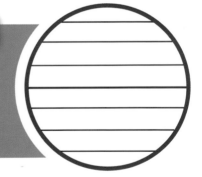

South Pole

the southernmost point on Earth; the South Pole lies in Antarctica

longitude lines

(LON-ji-tood)—imaginary lines that run from the North Pole to the South Pole and help show position; the prime meridian is the longitude line that is the starting point for measuring distance east and west

Australia

Australia is the smallest continent. Surrounded by water, it is home to many plants and animals that are found nowhere else on Earth. Much of Australia is wild, very dry, and deserted. Most of Australia's people live in the continent's large cities.

Great Dividing Range

a long chain of low mountains in eastern Australia; divides the dry inner part of the continent from the coastline

desert

an area of very dry land; Australia has a number of hot, sandy deserts; deserts can also be cold and covered in ice

Ayers Rock

a huge flat-top rock of red sandstone in the middle of the Australian continent; indigenous Australians call it "Uluru" and consider it holy

AUSTRALIA

Southern Ocean

Murray River

the longest river in Australia; flows south 1,200 miles (1,931 kilometers) from the Australian Alps to the Southern Ocean

Tasmania

an island state of Australia that lies south of the continent

Oceania

a group of countries surrounding and including Australia; New Zealand, Papua New Guinea, and Tahiti are three of the 14 island countries in Oceania

Simpson Desert

a very dry desert in the middle of Australia; usually receives less than 5 inches (127 millimeters) of rain each year

island

an area of land that is surrounded by water; Australia is an island

Great Barrier Reef

the world's largest coral reef at about 1,250 miles (2,012 km) long; coral is a hard material made up of the skeletons of tiny sea animals

Great Victoria Desert

a huge desert in southwestern Australia; covered in red sand hills, grasses, and saltwater areas called marshes

Australian Alps

a group of mountains at the southern end of the Great Dividing Range; the highest peak is Mount Kosciuszko, which stands 7,313 feet (2,229 meters)

outback

a wild and mostly deserted area of Australia

indigenous peoples

groups of people who have a long history of living in a particular area; the world has about 300 million indigenous groups; Australia's groups have lived on the continent for more than 45,000 years

kangaroo

an Australian animal with large ears, strong back legs, and a long, powerful tail; kangaroos are marsupials, meaning that after birth, they grow inside a pouch of skin on their mother's belly

koala

a furry, tree-climbing Australian animal that eats only eucalyptus; like kangaroos, koalas are marsupials

eucalyptus

(yoo-kuh-LIP-tuhss)—a type of tall evergreen tree that comes from Australia; the tree's strong-smelling oil is often used in perfumes and health products

wattle

a heat-loving shrub or tree with ball-shaped clusters of white or yellow flowers; also known as an acacia plant; the golden wattle is Australia's national flower

emu

a large Australian bird with a long neck, shaggy feathers, and a big beak; emus cannot fly, but they can run up to 30 miles (48 km) per hour

budgerigar

(BUHJ-uh-ree-gahr)—a small Australian parrot; wild budgerigars are usually bright green with a yellow head

export

to send goods for sale from one country to another; Australia exports more coal than any other country in the world

Europe

Europe is the second-smallest continent. It is separated from Africa by the Mediterranean Sea. The Black Sea, the Caspian Sea, and the Ural Mountains separate it from Asia. Many kinds of people, plants, and animals call this small continent home.

Scandinavia

an area of northern Europe made up of the countries of Norway, Sweden, and Denmark

Norway
Sweden
Baltic Sea
North Sea
Denmark
Russia
ASIA
England
EUROPE
Ukraine
Germany
Atlantic Ocean
France
Romania
Black Sea
Caspian Sea
Bulgaria
Italy
Adriatic Sea
Aegean Sea
ASIA
Spain
Greece
Mediterranean Sea
AFRICA

Baltic Sea

a body of brackish water that borders nine northern European countries; brackish water is saltier than fresh water, but not as salty as seawater

Balkan Peninsula

an area of land in southeastern Europe surrounded by the Black Sea, the Adriatic Sea, and the Aegean Sea; 11 countries share the peninsula, including Greece, Bulgaria, and Romania

Meseta

(may-SAY-tuh)—a dry, windy, highlands area that covers much of central Spain; the mountains of the Meseta are flat-topped

Danube River

a major river that flows 1,770 miles (2,849 km) from Germany to the Black Sea; touches 18 European countries

Alps

a long, crescent-shaped mountain range in south-central Europe; Mont Blanc, which stands 15,771 feet (4,807 m), is the highest peak in the Alps

Italian Peninsula

a long, boot-shaped piece of land that lies between the Mediterranean Sea and the Adriatic Sea; home to the country of Italy

Volga River

Europe's longest river at 2,290 miles (3,685 km) and the main waterway of western Russia

Mediterranean Sea

a large body of water that separates Europe from Africa; connects to the Atlantic Ocean on the west by a narrow waterway called the Strait of Gibraltar

English Channel

a narrow body of water that separates England from France; also connects the Atlantic Ocean to the North Sea

11

roe deer

a medium-sized red-brown deer found in the forests of Europe and Asia

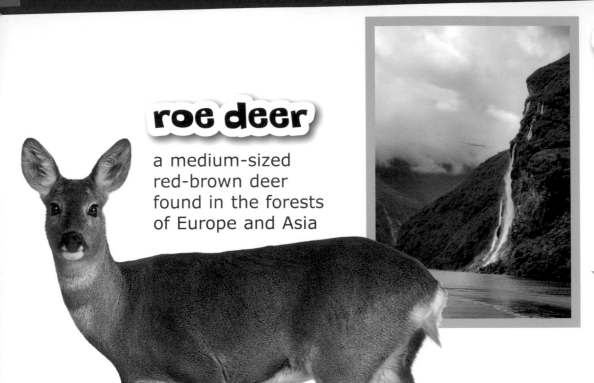

fjord

a long, narrow waterway that forms an inlet along a coastline; fjords have steep walls of land on both sides and are found mostly along the western coast of Norway

Acropolis

a rocky hillside above Athens, Greece, on which a number of ancient buildings stand; the most famous is the Parthenon, built in honor of the Greek goddess Athena

tundra

an area of flat or nearly flat land in the far northern parts of the world, such as northern Scandinavia; because the ground is always frozen, few trees grow on the tundra

Roman Colosseum

an ancient stadium-like building in Rome, Italy; it was largely used to stage battles between men called gladiators

canal

a waterway built by humans and used for travel; Venice, Italy, is a European city famous for its canals

European polecat

a member of the weasel family; polecats live in the woods, sleeping during the day and hunting at night

coniferous tree

any tree that grows cones and thin, pointed leaves called needles; common throughout Europe

Antarctica

Antarctica lies in the southernmost part of the world. It is the third-smallest continent and the world's largest desert. Only a handful of scientists live there. The sun never rises in the winter. It never sets in the summer. The temperature usually stays below freezing.

Southern Ocean

ANTARCTICA

Transantarctic Mountains

a mountain range that divides western Antarctica from eastern Antarctica

glacier

(GLAY-shur)—a huge, slow-moving sheet of ice; much of Antarctica is covered by glaciers

ice shelf

a chunk of ice that is partly floating in water and partly connected to land; Antarctica's Ross Ice Shelf is the largest floating piece of ice in the world

Antarctic midge

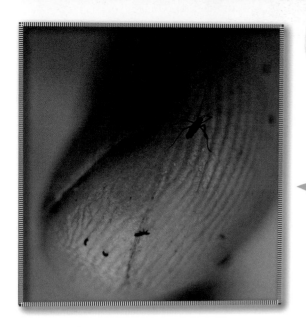

a tiny, wingless insect; one of the few creatures that lives in Antarctica year-round

lichen

(LYE-ken)—a flat, mossy, plantlike organism that grows on rocks and other solid surfaces; one of the few things that can grow in Antarctica's cold, dry climate

McMurdo Station

a base camp for scientists studying Antarctica; the largest science center on the continent

Antarctic icefish

a pale fish with no red blood cells (its blood is clear); the most common fish living in the freezing waters of the Southern Ocean

emperor penguin

a large black and white bird with gold streaks on its head; the largest of all penguins, standing about 4 feet (122 centimeters) tall; wild emperors live only in Antarctica

South America

South America is the world's fourth-largest continent. It is home to a great variety of plant and animal life. It's also home to hundreds of indigenous groups. In addition to the Amazon rain forest, the continent has wide grasslands, lots of coastline, and some of the world's tallest mountains.

Andes Mountains

the longest mountain range on land and one of the world's tallest; stretches 5,500 miles (8,851 km) along the western coast of South America, from Colombia to the southern tip of the continent

Valdes Peninsula

a large chunk of land that juts out into the Atlantic Ocean; serves as a wildlife protection place for many kinds of animals, including southern right whales and elephant seals

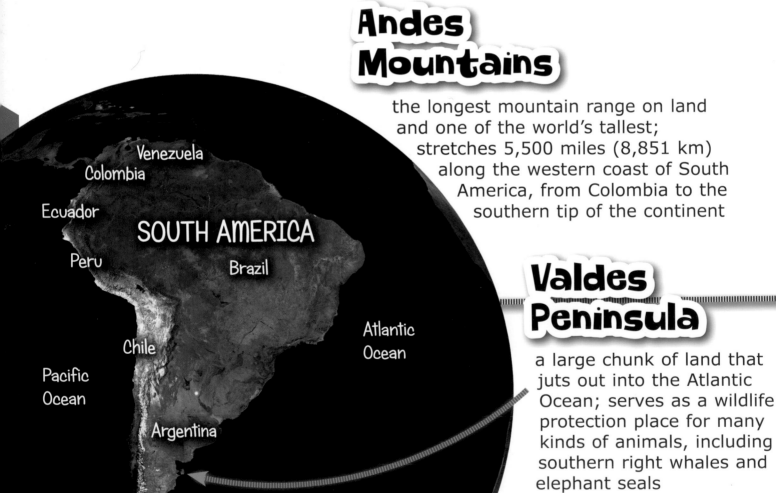

Venezuela
Colombia
Ecuador
SOUTH AMERICA
Peru
Brazil
Chile
Atlantic Ocean
Pacific Ocean
Argentina

Mount Aconcagua

(ah-kuhn-KAH-gwah)—the tallest mountain in the western hemisphere, standing 22,831 feet (6,959 m); part of the southern Andes Mountains

Atacama Desert

the driest desert in the world; lies in Chile, stretching from the Pacific Ocean to high in the cold Andes Mountains

Pantanal

the world's largest freshwater wetlands; lies mostly in Brazil; very hot and humid

rain forest

thick forestlands that get heavy rainfall every year; although most common along the equator, rain forests can also be found in cooler areas of the world; rain forest trees stay green year-round

Galápagos Islands

a group of islands off the coast of Ecuador in the Pacific Ocean; home to many animals that live nowhere else, including the Galápagos giant tortoise and the marine iguana

llama

a shaggy, long-necked animal related to the camel family; used in South American mountains as sturdy pack animals

Machu Picchu

an area of deserted ruins high in the Andes Mountains of Peru; built long ago by the Inca people; unknown to outsiders until 1911

rubber tree

a common rain forest tree; rubber tree sap is used to make tires and other rubber products

Amazon rain forest

the largest tropical (hot) rain forest in the world, measuring about 2.1 million square miles (5.4 million square kilometers); home to millions of kinds of plants and animals

pampas

wide, mostly treeless grasslands in South America, east of the Andes Mountains, primarily in Argentina

leafcutter ant

a rain forest insect with strong jaws; like farmers, leafcutter ants grow their own food

Amazon River

the longest river in South America and the second-longest river in the world; flows about 4,000 miles (6,437 km), from the Andes Mountains to the Atlantic Ocean

cacao

(kuh-KAH-oh)—a small evergreen tree found in tropical parts of South America; seeds of the cacao tree are used to make cocoa and chocolate

Angel Falls

the world's tallest waterfall; located in Venezuela, the waterfall drops 3,212 feet (979 m)

Native American

a member of a group of peoples who have lived in the North, South, and Central Americas since before European explorers arrived

Inca

a group of Native American people who lived in South America long ago; the Incas thrived in Peru and throughout the Andes Mountains until their kingdom died away in the mid-1500s

North America

North America is the world's third-largest continent. With its mountain ranges, wide plains, hot deserts, and frozen soil, it's also a land of differences. It's the only continent that has every type of climate.

Greenland

the world's largest island that is not a continent; lies between the Atlantic Ocean and the Arctic Ocean and is almost completely covered in ice; part of Denmark

Central America

a long, narrow piece of North America that connects to South America; seven countries lie in Central America: Belize, Guatemala, El Salvador, Honduras, Nicaragua, Costa Rica, and Panama

Arctic Ocean

United States

Canada

NORTH AMERICA

United States

Atlantic Ocean

Gulf of Mexico

Mexico

Caribbean Sea

SOUTH AMERICA

Rocky Mountains

a collection of about 100 separate mountain groups that runs from northwestern Canada through the western United States

Grand Canyon

a wide, deep rock valley with steep sides in the southwestern United States; formed more than 6 million years ago by the Colorado River

Mount McKinley

the tallest mountain in North America, standing 20,320 feet (6,194 m); also known as Denali; located in the extreme northwestern United States

Appalachian Mountains

a major mountain range in eastern North America that runs from Canada to the southern United States

Death Valley

a hot desert in the southwestern United States; the lowest, driest, and hottest place on the continent

Great Plains

a wide flatland area covering western parts of Canada and the United States; grass-covered with few trees

moose

a large member of the deer family found mainly in North America; male moose grow big, flat horns called antlers

deciduous tree

(dih-SIJ-oo-uhs)—a tree that drops its leaves every year in the fall; maples, oaks, and elms are common deciduous trees in North America

Great Lakes

a group of five large freshwater lakes between Canada and the United States; the lakes are Superior, Michigan, Huron, Erie, and Ontario

Colorado River

one of North America's longest and most important rivers; called the "lifeline of the Southwest," the Colorado supplies water to the dry southwestern part of the continent

Inuit

a Native American group living in the Canadian Arctic, Greenland, and parts of the extreme northwestern United States

volcano

an opening in Earth's surface that sometimes sends out hot lava, steam, and ash; the United States has 50 active volcanoes

Mississippi River

North America's longest river, flowing 2,350 miles (3,782 km) from near the Canada-U.S. border to the Gulf of Mexico

Maya

a Native American group living mostly in southern Mexico and northern Central America; had a highly developed way of life that reached its peak about 1,750 to 1,100 years ago

Gulf of Mexico

a large body of water that opens to the Atlantic Ocean on the southeastern edge of North America; the United States curves around the gulf's northern side, while Mexico borders its western and southern sides

gila monster

(HEE-lah)—a large poisonous lizard found in the deserts of Mexico and the southwestern United States

Caribbean Islands

a group of thousands of islands in the Caribbean Sea that stretches southeast from the Gulf of Mexico to the waters north of South America

Africa

A land of sand dunes, tropical forests, and grasslands, Africa is the world's second-largest continent. More than 1 billion people call Africa home. This number includes about 3,000 ethnic groups. More than 2,000 languages are spoken on the African continent.

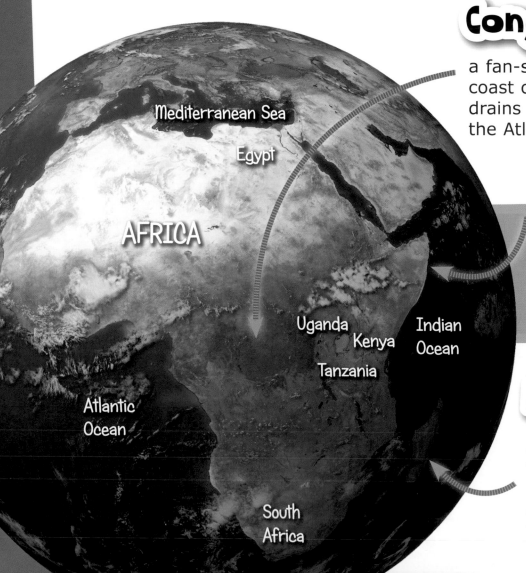

Mediterranean Sea

Egypt

AFRICA

Uganda
Kenya
Tanzania
Indian Ocean

Atlantic Ocean

South Africa

Congo Basin

a fan-shaped area on the western coast of Africa; the Congo River drains water from the basin into the Atlantic Ocean

Horn of Africa

a piece of land in eastern Africa that juts out into the Indian Ocean; forms a sharp point that looks like a horn

Madagascar

a small island nation off the eastern coast of Africa; lemurs (furry, monkey-like animals with long, ringed tails) come from the island

Sahara Desert

the world's largest hot desert; 3.3 million square miles (8.5 million sq km), covering almost all of northern Africa

Mount Kilimanjaro

the tallest mountain in Africa at 19,340 feet (5,895 m); lies in Tanzania, near the border of Kenya

Lake Victoria

the largest lake in Africa; lies in the countries of Uganda, Tanzania, and Kenya

Nile River

the world's longest river at 4,184 miles (6,733 km); flows south to north through northeastern Africa and empties into the Mediterranean Sea

Victoria Falls

a very broad waterfall in southern Africa; often called the "smoke that thunders" because of the misty water and its loud roar as it falls

Cape of Good Hope

a rocky piece of land at the tip of southern Africa; an area of rough seas and many storms

Ngorongoro Crater

(nuh-GRON-gah-roh)—a large, deep bowl-shaped area in northern Tanzania; part of the Ngorongoro Conservation Area, which is home to black rhinos, lions, wildebeest, zebras, and other wildlife

ethnic group

a group of people who share qualities such as language or religion; two of Africa's best-known ethnic groups are the Zulu people (South Africa) and the Masai people (eastern Africa)

savanna

a flat area of grassland with few trees; found in warm parts of the world, such as Africa

baobab tree

(BOW-bab)—a fruit-bearing tree from Africa with a very thick trunk

cheetah

a member of the cat family commonly found in southern Africa; the world's fastest land animals, they can run up to 75 miles (121 km) per hour

migration

the movement of a group of people or animals from one place to another; more than 1 million wildebeest migrate each year in eastern Africa in search of food and water

Great Pyramid of Giza

the biggest, most famous, and oldest of three very large pyramids in El Giza, Egypt; pyramids once served as tombs for Egyptian kings and queens

African elephant

a large gray animal with a long trunk, large ears, and tusks; the world's largest land animal; most wild African elephants live in South Africa

Asia

Asia covers more of the planet than any other continent. This largest continent is home to the tallest mountains on land and the largest object ever built by human hands. It's also home to the largest number of people—more than 4 billion!

Dead Sea

one of the world's saltiest bodies of water; the Dead Sea is 10 times saltier than any ocean; very few living things can survive there

Southwest Asia

a group of countries that lies between northern Africa and south-central Asia; part of Egypt, Saudi Arabia, Turkey, Iran, and many smaller countries are part of Southwest Asia

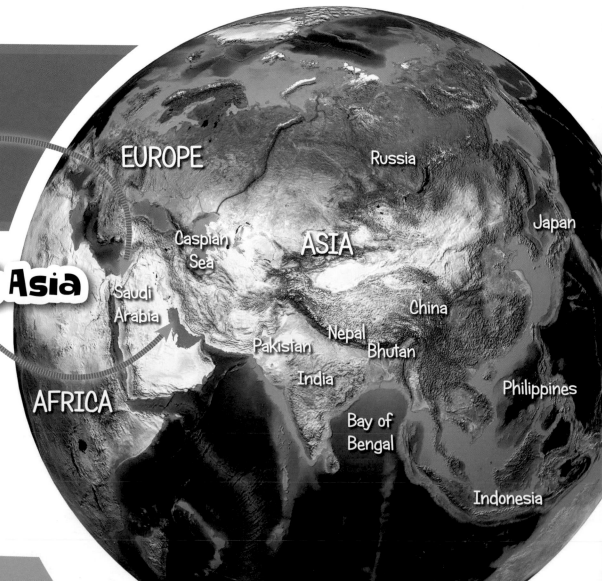

EUROPE

Russia

Japan

Caspian Sea

ASIA

Saudi Arabia

China

Nepal

Pakistan

Bhutan

India

Philippines

AFRICA

Bay of Bengal

Indonesia

Himalayas

the world's tallest mountain range; the Himalayas stretch across the countries of Pakistan, India, China, Nepal, and Bhutan; the word "Himalaya" means "home of the snow" in the Urdu language

Mount Everest

the tallest mountain peak in the world at 29,028 feet (8,848 m); part of the Himalayas

Lake Baikal

(bye-KAHL)—the oldest and deepest lake in the world, located in Russia; about 25 million years old

Gobi Desert

a wide, rocky, cold desert in northern Asia; "Gobi" means "waterless place" in the Mongolian language

Ganges River

(GAN-jeez)—the longest river in India flows from the Himalayas to the Bay of Bengal; said to be holy by people of the Hindu religion

Caspian Sea

the world's largest body of water surrounded on all sides by land; marks the border between Asia and southeastern Europe

crude oil

a natural liquid from which gas and other fuels are made; most of the world's crude oil is found in Asia

Ural Mountains

a mountain range that runs north and south, roughly marking the border between Asia and Europe; hundreds of millions of years old

giant panda

a large, bamboo-eating black-and-white animal from China belonging to the bear family; only about 1,600 giant pandas still live in the wild

bamboo

a plant with long, hollow stems found mostly in the southern hemisphere

tiger

a big gold-and-black-striped member of the cat family; now found mostly in India; wild tigers are an endangered species

Yangtze River

(yang-SEE)—the longest river in Asia and the third-largest river in the world, flowing 3,915 miles (6,301 km) through China; "Yangtze" means "long river" in Chinese

Taj Mahal

(TAHZH muh-HAHL)—a grand palace in Agra, India, built by an Indian ruler to honor his wife; took 22 years to build and was finished in 1653

Great Wall of China

an ancient stone wall in northern China; 12,427 miles (20,000 km) long, the wall is the largest object ever built by human hands; work began in 220 BC and lasted for almost 2,000 years

taiga

(TYE-guh)—cold forestland areas found in Asia, northern Europe, and North America; evergreens (trees that stay green all year) are the most common taiga trees

mangrove tree

a tree with large, exposed roots that grows in or near warm salty water; mangrove forests are common in Southeast Asia

Read More

Gibson, Karen Bush. *Spotlight on Europe.* Spotlight on the Continents. Mankato, Minn.: Capstone Press, 2011.

Kalman, Bobbie, and Rebecca Sjonger. *Explore Asia.* Explore the Continents. New York: Crabtree Pub. Co., 2007.

Sepehri, Sandy. *Continents.* Landforms. Vero Beach, Fla.: Rourke Pub., 2008.

Titles in this set:

Show Me
COMMUNITY HELPERS

Show Me
THE CONTINENTS

Show Me
DINOSAURS

Show Me
DOGS

Show Me
INSECTS

Show Me
POLAR ANIMALS

Show Me
REPTILES

Show Me
ROCKS AND MINERALS

Show Me
SPACE

Show Me
TRANSPORTATION

Show Me
THE UNITED STATES

Show Me
THE U.S. PRESIDENCY

Internet Sites

FactHound offers a safe, fun way to find Internet sites related to this book. All of the sites on FactHound have been researched by our staff.

Here's all you do:

Visit *www.facthound.com*

Type in this code: 9781476501147

Check out projects, games and lots more at
www.capstonekids.com